LIFTED TO THE WIND

LIFTED TO THE WIND

POEMS 1974 - 2015

SUSAN GARDNER

RED MOUNTAIN PRESS

Many poems in this book have been previously published, several in altered form. The author gratefully acknowledges

"Each One," *Veils, Halos and Shackles: International Poems on the Abuse and Oppression of Women.* Charles Fishman and Smita Sahay, editors, Kasva Press, (forthcoming), anthology.

"Canción vespertina ~ Evensong," *200 New Mexico Poems: 100 Poems Celebrating the Past, 100 More for the Future, an Official Project of the New Mexico Centennial.* Lisa Hase-Jackson, editor, (forthcoming), anthology.

"Home Bound," *Lummox #2.* R.D. Anderson, editor, 2013, anthology.

"French Chocolate," *Wine, Cheese and Chocolate: A Taste of Literary Elegance.* Manzanita Writers Press, 2015, anthology.

"June Garden", *HOW TO....* Harwood Art Center, Albuquerque, New Mexico, 2012, anthology.

"First Flush El primero sonrojo," *The Four Seasons.* Kind of a Hurricane Press, A.J. Huffman and April Salzano, co-editors, 2015, anthology.

ISBN 978-0-9908047-4-1

Printed in the United States of America

RED MOUNTAIN PRESS
Santa Fe, New Mexico
www.redmountainpress.us

BY THE SAME AUTHOR

To Inhabit the Felt World 2013

Drawing the Line ~ A Passionate Life 2011

Box of Light ~ Caja de Luz: Poems in English and Spanish 2008

Stone Music ~ The Art and Poetry of Susan Gardner 2007

Intimate Landscapes 1998

FOR RDR

DANCER
Sumi on handmade paper, 3 x 4.5 inches
2015

LOCKED GATE

On December 19, 1980
Alaíde Foppa went to buy flowers.
She disappeared.

Sixty-six years old.
In a cellar, in a bloody cell, in Guatemala,
by the hands of thugs.
Or worse.

I walk by Alaíde's sweet house in Tepoztlán
refuge from city noise and endless sorrow
   Mario, husband of decades, killed
     in Guatemala by a car
  two sons, Mario and Juan Pablo,
     Guatemalan guerillas, dead
     Silvia, belovéd hija, hiding in Cuba
     Laura and Julio, safe in an unquiet life
       in Mexico.

Alaída's house is closed.

   White cotton curtains cross the fastened windows,
     embroidered flowers near the sills.

Past the locked iron gate, leaves blow in corners
                    of the patio, brown on the stones
                    undisturbed.

Now and then, someone, thinking of Alaída, tosses a
                    message through the patterned bars
                    also undisturbed.

Thirty years ago I write a poem, lift it to the wind,
                    through the barred gate. Dust now.

Alaíde loved the light of Italian art
                    and the music of Italian words.

Teacher, translator, scholar,

          for almost half a century, she put words on paper

          justice equality honor beauty

          despair hope.

No body. No grave. Not a strand of hair.

Only paper reminds us

    of her beauty, her courage

but a century after she was born, her words,
    written down, are read.

Remembered, like Joe Hill, she's alive as you or me.

2015

Ricochet

At six o'clock the songs of swallows
spill themselves through the air
pushing themselves off imperturbable yellow stone walls.

Boulders, stuck fast forever, are disturbed in the echo.

Rebotar

A las seis de la tarde
las canciones de las golondrinas
se derrama a través del aire

se empúje afuera
de las paredes imperturbables de piedra amarilla.

Cantos rodados, atrapados para siempre,
están perturbados en el eco.

2003

MONTSERRAT REVISITED

November drizzle dismisses easy days
        sky fog belts rocky towers
        last tenacious yellow cleaves to sycamore

Wet cobbles cross the village
        past sienna-plastered walls
        to the arched church portal

High-window light falls on young faces
        eyes wide, open mouths release ordinary voices
        celestial in the stone space

Long aisles interrupted with chapels
        virgin heroines long departed
        kings, conquerors, redeemers

One new brilliant glass-doored space, punctuated with
                crossed hands, crossed feet,
                thorned corona
        to enter, hands push against the wooden bar
        caress the carved history of Catalunya

Gentle-voiced crowd edges around the perimeter
        up sloped steps scooped out by each pilgrim's foot
        the black Madonna, centuries of candled
        smoke and love shine on her face

Long promenade, black iron choirs
      fat, thin, tall, short,
      red, green, white wax pillars
flame with hope

Outside people are passing by one more door.

Red walls, shining wood floor, bright lights,
a room full of things

          two long white glowing wedding dresses
          sequins, embroidery, gathered stitching
          cover silk petticoats and sheer linings

          black sleeves touch white silk
          a very short suit of black wool
          young brother to accompany the bride?
          stranger?

Brass hooks hold
      small shoes
      plastic flowers
      infant's yellow bib
      summery straw hat
          with silk flowers around the crown

tiny girl's starched pink dress
white rickrack pristine
no dribbles from a meal of applesauce

Past the corner more hooks
a shelf with
    baskets
    music box
    chest with dark red velvet lining

Round another corner
    more flowers
    toys, photographs
    crutches

    sorrows
    gratitude

A sign says
    everything
        all the objects
    are left behind

    and may yet be reclaimed

2012

COLD RIVER

The river runs cold now
flavored with last year's ice.

Around water-soft rocks
it pools clean and frigid

rushing
on its way
to oceanic immortality

to oblivion.

RIO FRESCO

El río corre helado ahora
con el sabor del hielo del año pasado.

Alrededor de las rocas, suavizadas por el agua,
se estanca limpio y frío

precipitándose
en su camino
hacia inmortalidad oceánica

hacia olvido.

2007

EACH ONE

I

Men drive the jitney buses.

Bus girls
      collect tickets on board
      clean the buses
      perform other services

from poor farms indentured for a few years
      to get the family through hard times
      or escape the soul-scarring country grind

in the city, they live in a company dormitory, each
      room with sixty girls
      paid very low wages
      ten hour days, six days a week

constant abuse from riders
harassment from drivers, sexual favors demanded or
      taken
      there on the rubber matted black floor of the
      bus

uneducated, rough-spoken, dirty, unwilling, unpaid
      prostitutes

after five years, at eighteen or nineteen years old,
    the bus company
    is to provide a dowry
    for entry into married indenture

II

Summer afternoon at the YWCA, sixteen women
    in pale, starched, linen dresses,
    meet in a bare, dusty room
    sun slanting in through open windows

folding chairs in a circle,
    we eat watermelon
    suck ice
    ask

who are these girls
what do these ragamuffins
    dirty, loud, rank-smelling
have to do with us?

we know the sorrow of
our younger sisters

each one does one thing
to assuage our outrage
quiet our shame

each one
        our sisters, ourselves
        grows one iota

toward a free life

2013

LOW VISIBILITY

No moon lights the way
     breath in the cold air
    just visible —
        clouds rising to the clouds.

We guess where the road goes.

2006

HUMMING ROOM

I
Humming room
tube twists of plastic carry
        false pink of new blood
        the lie of another promise.

Eyes open round to compass the midnight crisis.
Inch long black hairs comma the white sheet.
No blue milk taste on lips or tongue. No tears
fall on falling lashes.

Muscles starve for oxygen.
Fingers unfist, swell, open.
Skin peels back
        fiery flesh
        too fragile to contain.

        Through roughened surface,
        the bloody serum
        seeps through blistered layers.

Breaths frail. Thread-thin muscles
do not lift the three inch ribs.

Cries whimper to silence.

White box, blue dress —
      less than one square yard of cotton to keep
      the brown dirt at bay.

Rotted together now.
Dirt. Dress. Girl.

II

Quiet room
dark table with fat legs

      box big enough
      to hold a family's picnic

            standing in sunshine
            speechless.

Hearts beat strong. Lungs
breathe

air you will never need. Brothers
cannot remember
your disappeared face.

My beloved
we are silent.

III
Memory's shape

With no other proof but memory exists
                              that moon blue eye.

Black curl creeps over the edge of an ear.
Smile commits nothing more — or less —
                              than this moment.

Trust an untrustworthy future

201

PYRE

struggle, resist, gasp
to leave, defy necessity
renitent, obdurate

mouth forms an O, tastes air,
eyes close, see only his long-ago face
skin tight over bone, wrinkleless

      radiant life-light pours out into air
      illuminates the passage

pyre's smoke steams to blue
    portion
        to clouds
        to rain
   measure
        small air

wash shards and ash of bone together
sink in earth   feed trees

return
      quaking yellow

tremble
      on our still faces

2012

TEA

Soft golden green
held by this shred of gentle burned earth,
smelling of hillsides and the sunrise
giving up the bitter-clean taste of the morning
silky light rises to warm me.

Holding sunlight forever
in tiny black bits
whispering in the darkness
longing to set free the golden being
it has been from the beginning.

1984

NEW YORK PUBLIC LIBRARY

A book connects us to one another through time and
space. We hold the author's ideas in our hand
unmediated by anything except our own curiosity.

I

The children's room
> five steps above the main floor
> open shelves for young patrons
> near the door librarian's desk

read pictures, read poems
> hushed rustle of pages
> dust motes in the window's sunlight shaft
> bindings across silk-smooth golden maple
> quiet clicks stamp dates on paper slips

Borrow armfuls of books

Five steps down, secreted from infant eyes
forbidden treasure

necessary whispers only
perfect

II

Marble beasts before limestone columns
allow passage
across hundreds of steps

    mimes mug for nickels
    anxious lovers suspended in anticipation of one face
    arms overflow with books unaligned

        scholars climb the white flights
        ernest heads bow with weight of words
        readers ascend to their shared home

III

Double-storied coffered domes over stacks,
    asylum for earth's every thought
    city's every scholar,
      idler, pencil-pusher,
      venerable, solitary,
      prized, repudiated
    aged and child
        have a place at this table

sounds brush through silent space,
      talk soft at the desk,
            pencils scribble,
            shoes cross marble floors
            index fingers slide under corners
                    impatient to turn pages
            everything we touch is paper

thoughts from yesterday and millennia before
seined in paged nets

on heads bent over books
brass lamps shine gold

            consolation for the lonely
            comfort for the cold
            solace for the bereft

stay until the midnight closing hour

2012

DEEP WATER

sun-stunned dark water
touches curved blue atmosphere
ultramarine horizon invisible

skin darkens in fevered summer air
sweat a salty sheen
black curls halo over reddening ears
legs stiff at water's boundary

plunge in, drown in brilliant delight
weightless, jubilant
float besotted

I learn to swim
2012

DICHOSO DÍA

Me metí en el agua profunda
me sumergí en ese brillate líquido limpio
deslumbrante en el sol.

Me ahogué en las sensaciones del verano
floté en éxtasis, ingrávida, jubilosa.
Aprendí a nadir..

1984

PAPER AND INK

Ink: blackest love
Paper: whitest host

Trees: living breathing green
          home for birds' songs
                    worms' lust

Cut blasted burned charred

Ready to accept the embrace of our words.

Paper: whitest host
Ink: blackest love

1984

Black ink on stone landscape
   violet Duan volcanic tuff, blue-black She slate,
   obsidian, soft, gray river rocks

clinging smell of charred carbon powder and glue
rumors of friction wearing at stick and stone

formless ink, boundless, becomes

   poem, book, pine branch painting
   letter of good-bye
   stain on the table.

Trees' living, long white cambium filaments

   cut, simmered, slurried
   held afloat
   in the warm bath

spill from the mold
onto old pine cousins in the sun

felt into paper.

A branchlet, trimmed, sanded, silk-tied

to badger and fox hairs,
soaked in rabbit glue, dripped clean,
straightforward.

Hand circles inside black boundary,
water reflects from black surface
ink blackens
marbles over inkstone

slowly, slowly readies itself for the brush.

The lake of blackness spreads over anthracite well of
grinding stone.

Ink pulled into paper,
inadvertent turnings

thickness varied by pressure applied
        onto each felted fiber
bleeds at the edges

Time lengthens

Brush relinquishes its charge,
sets free the ink it carries
to inhabit the felt world.

2012

Eye-shape bowl
     ringed dark around the iris
     periphery between color and air
Suspended within the apparent ivory-black
     flat black bands concentrate roundness
     border between light and no light

        viridian, carmine, cochineal
        cinnabar, miraculous red becomes green
        citrine, golden light of powdered gems
        cobalt, cerulean, indigo

Prussian blue, wanting red, Diesbach made sky
Hooker's green, for his perfect green leaves
Payne's gray, less black than black,
        precise tints seep through leaking light
Vermeer blue, precious pure lapis lazuli from Badakshan,
        blooming with lead

        umber, the smell of Italy's hillsides
        sienna, Tuscany's earth, moved to galleries
        lead, life to colors, death to artists
        paint linen geometry

Cézanne's eyes open to the shape of the world as it may be
2015

PURE WIND
24 x 60 inches
1983

WINTER

1983-2015

BREATH OF MERCY

Hard edged cold slides in
  ribs rigid, pleural sacs hold iced shards of air
    lungs freeze from inside out

  white fingernails roll over
    round reddened fingers
      on fire with cold
  burning cold runs through each phalanx of
    fingers and toes
    lodges in stiff knuckles immovable
        in frozen jackets of useless
    ligaments

rime of sleep wraps tight
  eyelids droop
  sparkles of crimson, cobalt, citrine
  warm the last slivers of fading, euphoric mind

NEBRASKA SUNRISE

On the verge of a pond, grass glimmers with rime.
Thin ice cracks in tatters as the temperature rises a few degrees.
Early cold sunlight seeps across the eastern plain
And lends its energy to the half-frozen water.
New mists vaporize in a minute
Like crushed diamonds
Rising on the still silent air
Awakening the loons.

SNOWY DAY

over pale summits no reflection
only motionless pewter sky

last year's piñon branches burn
resin scent traces through cold

at the window first flakes
on already fat lilac buds

drink chamomile tea
don't work, read poetry

sleep in the snowy fog

CHILLY

I am used to my solitude
surrounding me like an old quilt
keeping me almost warm enough
on this cold night

FRIOLENTA

Estoy acostumbrada a mi soledad
envolviéndome como un viejo edredón
dándome un calor casi suficiente
en esta noche fría

COLD BLUE

blue scraps of sky
crack out clouds

dull winter ground
rigid brown

soon
snow we've longed for

STORM

clouds bank black against less black mountains
flying snow crosses dusky sun
fractured into winter rainbow

SPRING

1985-2015

BRETON DAY

Up past the atmosphere
steaming breath and steaming coast

ahead, banks, piles, mountains of air
meet streaming foggy sky

rough edged clouds remember
the cold sea where they were born

Drizzle pours sheets of soft rain
descends over the garden

cloudy rain rolls low on the landscape
watery sunshine inundated again

Above the pitching, stretching ocean of cloud
sky is suddenly blue, aglow in high afternoon light

so brilliant you have to squint
or turn away for just a moment

All day every molecule drinks its fill

Stinging tiny droplets pass in windy torrents
lift again, make room for mists of morning

At ten o'clock daylight fades
clouds wreathe the moon

CHANGE OF SEASON

Waterfall
falling
water
running down the cheeks of the hills

Coldspring
spring
rain
fallen into the cleft of the rock

Airspray
air
sprays of icy fragrance

Tears blown over the sky

FIRST FLUSH

Mountains flush with dawn frost
blossoms of magenta
then scarlet
crimson lake
chlorophyll not yet overwhelming first leaflets

EL PRIMERO SONROJO

Las montañas colmadas
de la helada del amanecer
flores de magenta
escarlata,
carmesí lago
la clorofila no abruma las primeras hojillas todavía

CLEMENT

this fine rainy day
clouds scud in wind
chase isobars of cold across
iced spring jet stream

EARLY HARVEST

tomato blossoms explode
in yellow dismay

silky flames flare
in icy rain

FROZEN BLOOM

overnight
virgin pinks shrivel to brown
moonlit frost

fertility lost
to cold April

TORONTO ISLAND EARLY MORNING

clouds rest on grassy ground

no shadows cast
no darkness mars the light
no glint amends silent morning

SUMMER

1975-2015

Summer Idyll

One note from a child's flute
Resting on the air
Like a swallow on the porch rail

Rain in Santa Clara

As the wind crosses the mesa
leaves twist silvergreen to greet the rain.

On this hot afternoon all faces turn toward the skyfall
over Santa Clara.

Thunder rolls its baritone song nearby
but not here.

We are left with the sweet smell of ozone and
dampness.

STONE MUSIC

In a pond summer rain is falling.
The black stones, worn smooth in the stream,
click against each other
in our pockets

MÚSICA DE PIEDRA

En un estanque cae la lluvia veraniega
Las piedras negras, lisas en el arroyo,
chasquean,
            uno contra el otro,
en nuestros bolsillos

IN A POND, SUMMER RAIN
Sumi on paper, 9.5 x 10.25 inches
1975

MIDNIGHT BLUES

The heat has reawakened
an army of flies.
Unwillingly I stay awake

and see the moon set.

AUGUST

the meadow alight
cicadas brush their wings in desperate lust
a dark-haired girl stops for a moment
listening to the shadows

JUNE GARDEN

Hardy perennial lilies
do not need lifting.
Tall and graceful,
they like the sun.
They are dependable year after year.

Peonies are slow to take hold
but once established
live in their beds
for centuries.

Iris quite quickly
have great masses of beauty
but must be uprooted from time to time
or die of exuberance.

Humid night air

At this hour, before sunrise,
empty and without colors,
the invisible grass is touched
only by dew

Húmedo aire nocturno

En la hora antes del alba
vacía y sin colores
la hierba invisible
es tocada
sólo por el roci

FLAT AIR

The flat air,
white in the heat,
holds immobile
the weight of this afternoon.

The sun has captured the whole world
in its net of red light.

EL AIRE BLANCO

El aire sin dimensión,
blanco en el calor,
tiene inmóvil
el peso de esta tarde.

El sol ha capturado el mundo entero
en su red de luz roja.

VIRGA

Shy rain in the sky
falling toward us
hesitating
darkening the dusty day

VIRGA

Lluvia tímida en el cielo
cae hacia nosotros
vacilante
oscureciendo el día polvoroso

FULL MOON

Last night

a bird crossed in the path of moonlight.

The shadow ran over the white wall

and was lost in the window.

FALL

1985-2015

FOR LOVE OF RED

Red silk wet on pine needles.
Maple and sumac glimmer red against the road
neither as red as the red wool blanket
in my blue room.

Galaxy

In West Virginia red stripes of afternoon
meet the evening over village novas.

Each point in new dark
shines strands of light one to another.

The last of winter afternoon
glitters on past summer fertility,

ignites geometry of frozen irrigation
circles inside square girdles.

Ponds, still now,
show the last motion of fall.

Towns, hamlets, farms, stars reborn each night

blue and green light
against the newly black sky
and blacker night.

Vivid orange-yellow beacons
brush bold

against the winter ground

glow white with halogen
some sharp as points
some a little blurred in the center.

Still a trace of red sky beyond the grounded world.

GREEN BAMBOO

Imperceptible wind
moves long green bamboo leaves
across old black bark —
an inky brush in the Spanish air.

This almost tropical grass
bending to the ground
is cousin to upright bright Korean stalks.

Now in October

      ready to give up their green life
      for the leafless windy winter.

EVENSONG

Coyote families sing to each other in the dusk
    sun flares redden mountains
    sky blue as lapis lazuli
until moonless black night uncovers stars.

VESPERTINA

Las familias de coyotes se cantan al anochercer
    las llamaradas del sol enrojecen las montañas
    ciel azul como lapislázuli
hasta negro – sin luna – descubre las estrellas.

LAPSE OF MEMORY

Yellowing leaves murmur in the sun
brush the cool autumn dust
in small clouds

forgetful of the humid summer

LAPSUS

Las hojas amarillentas murmuran bajo el sol
rozando el polvo fresco del otoño
en nubes diminutas

olvidadizas del verano húmedo

Maple leaf

A maple leaf blazes through the day
and falls to rest
on a stone in the stream

Red twig

Morning fog lifts its wet weight,
red twig shines
in remembrance.

Clouds in a prism of urgency
rush to the sea.

An insect passes
lost in last summer's litter.

FOG

in deepening dusk
fog slides over the roof
shapeless
colors hidden

rain falls through fog
soundless over the stones

fog shrouds forest mouse
somewhere near   a song

IRON VENT, PARIS
Digital photograph, 6 x 8 inches
2012

WAR SUITE

1986-2013

THEY ALL SAY SO

All of them,
Romans, Goths, Visigoths
Saxons, Anglos, Vikings
Persians and Medes
Vedas and Mongols
Hans and Xings

On and on
they all say

"Mine is bigger than yours. "

Presbyterian Hindus
Buddhist Catholics
Zoroastrian Jews
Taoist
Realist
Idealists

On and on
they all say

"Mine is bigger than yours. "
SO?

2010

Sun tomorrow
> followed by cloudy days
> then rain

Breezy conditions
> small craft warnings
> large lakes advisory

> turbulence in the upper atmosphere

Any time is the time
to go to war.

2008

CONDICIONES DESESTABILIZADAS

Soleado mañana
seguido por días nebulosos
después lluvia

condiciones ventosas
advertencias a barcos pequeños
avisos en los lagos grandes

turbulencia en la atmósfera alta

Cualquier tiempo es el tiempo
de hacer la guerra.

2008

FEVER

Hot faces
Hot words
Fever of hate
Fire in the blood

Shoot hack rip rape
Slash burn bomb

What else can you do?
What else can we do?

2007

WHERE THE FLOWERS HAVE GONE
Armistice Day 11 Nov 2004

Wreaths of roses blood red
garlands of chrysanthemums
more yellow than the sun.

talk of honor
talk of sacrifice
talk of harm's way

then shoot.

2004

A DONDE SE FUERON LAS FLORES
Día del Armisticio 11 noviembre 2004

Coronas de rosas de rojo de sangre
guirnaldas de crisantemos
más amarillos que el sol

palabras de honor
palabras de sacrificio
palabras de la patria

después
disparen.

2004

DESIDERATA

Desperate want.

     To wake you at dawn,
          hands aflame, tongue fervent,
          skin blood burnished

          slake morning thirst with your sweet sweat
          scrawl my desires on your skin
          write my name on your mind.

     I want you to look at me in the dark
          see me here
          reborn

Body hungers.

     Lips still, tongue fat, ears cold,
     I want to stay
     a while longer
          evade the desolation of your absence
          evoke your ghost to stroke skin, caress breast,

assuage scorched spirit.

To hold and have without end
your face in my hands

A great eagle
keen talons outstretched

soars over.

2012

THE EAGLE

For a little while longer
I wanted to stay with you

      feel your smile
      see myself in your eyes
      enjoy the touch of your square hands

And for a little while longer
I wanted to evade the sadness
that, like a great, free eagle,
soars over my heart

1986

EL ÁGUILA

Por un poco más de tiempo
quería quedarme contigo

    sentir tu sonrisa
    verme en tus ojos
    disfrutarme en el roce
    de tus manos cuadradas

Y por un poco más de tempo
quería evitar la tristeza que,
como un águila noble y libre,
se cerne sobre mi corazón

2007

GOOD-BYE

I wanted to tell you everything
but I said nothing at all

I left in silence
  everything that was important
  everything my heart held
  everything the spirit wanted to shout

I hoped that you would understand
  by a kiss
  by a touch

The feelings
reborn each time I saw you

You left
and I could only say,
in a low voice,

good-by

1987

ADIÓS

Quería decirtelo todo
pero no dije nada

Dejé todo en silencio
       todo lo que era importante
       todo lo que mi corazón contenía
       todo lo que el espíritu quería gritar

Esperaba que tú entendieras
       con un beso
       con una carisia

Los sentimientos
renacían cada vez que volvía a verte

Te marchaste
y todo lo que pude decirte
sólo, en voz baja,
fue

adiós

1987

SNAKE IN THE GRASS
Sumi on handmade paper, 26 x 37
1984

SECOND SERPENT
Sumi on handmade paper, 26 x 37
1984

GARDEN BENCH

I

Narrowing path

    overrun with elephant ears, birds-of-paradise,
    pampas grass, plumed with decay.

    Tentacles avid, relentlessly accelerate.
    Sumptuous excess silences slow wind.

    In trees' canopy leaves reach for sky.

Alone here, unlonely,
immolant joy.

Between seasons, angled apart, the stone rests
on gray schist legs.

Each dry winter, cemented
    in their shrunken rigid waterless bed
        desiccated stems flake to dust.
        Leaves of streamside trees
        wait for July rain to decompose.

Each rainy summer night it sinks another iota
        toward its ancestral home
            amidst the bedrock
            of the river's underground channel
            tipping imperceptibly
            aslant in the slippery loam.

The path, a dirt track, no longer wide enough
        for two people to pass,

    once planted, now wild

            below steep rock steps a derelict fountain,
            verdigris-bronze head on the wall
            calcified mouth unable to spout the rainy runoff.

There the bench waited for decades.

Broken sun glints through heavy foliage.

Awake

I dream the afternoon.

Words fall through cascade of air.

Lines found in any order,
reordered,
folded away

found again
foundered in the torrent
found sheltered
this reader of stone in the rain.

II

Along a wide path

white with florescent light,
white with cold empty shining air
immaculate, pristine, precise,
five people, a crowd covered in antiseptic blue,
walk steady and resolute.

The tiny black mystery, size of a fingernail, sends out its life
      in threads, ready to take mine in suicidal excess.

      They, steadfast under blue lights, mean to murder
      this malignant monster.

Awake
      on the rolling platform
      I dream back this sheltered garden.

Silence and noise, garden leaves,
insects and wind, muffled footsteps.

          A stone in the river, washed smooth
          by twenty years absence,
          lies wet in the sunshine.

          Gentle in its muddy bed,
          heavy in my hand now, its body
          contains the igneous history of the world.

          A wader in this stream,
          I step in the icy flow and fall
          against its solid actuality.

2012-2013

THAT DAY

Knock your elbow against the edge of the door,
the funny bone will send a thrill of shock
right to your brain.

On this hot morning
our eyes knock.

In this instant
every bone funny
every muscle laughing
every hair breathless.

In the aftershock keep touching
that electric pain,

lean against the doorframe
until our hearts can move again.

1985

PHYSICS OF THE IRIS

Iris, courier of the gods, uses her rainbow
to carry messages between earth and heaven.

the body of one

raging with joy

against the surface of the other

in a cloud, as far apart

as infrared and ultraviolet

as hydrogen and oxygen

the spectrum broken open

electric songs

resounding

delirium of molecules let loose

critical mass achieved

Iris flying home with old news

2012

An old song told us to face the music and dance.

Moonlight and music and summer romance
were absent
when you rang the doorbell.

You said,
Hello,
in three notes,

your song rising, rolling a little
lower, ending with a raised eyebrow.

You said hello in three notes,
looping down to announce
you were here

Rising to ask
was I there?

Dancing came later.

2007

SUNDAY BREAKFAST

You woke this morning

meaning to smile

your eyes squinting in the glare of hoarse clouds.

You woke this morning

                    meaning to sing

wanting a great fall of trumpets

                    and beautiful brassy noise.

But your heart had laryngitis

and whispered a softer song instead.

So squinting and humming a little sharp

you made coffee

and toast with cheese and honey.

1985

A body wrapped around the sinuous space
      taut, shining
      full of air

Another, muscle and bone, air and water
      roused
      awake

One more, supple, stretched, reaching
      lifted high in expectation
      arching forward

In the last moment
poised over the voluptuous void, breathless
      they tremble, touch
      breaths coming together
become a single instrument

make music

2000

TOCANDO LA VIOLA

Un cuerpo envuelto alrededor del sinuoso espacio
    tenso, brillante
    lleno de aire

Otro, músculos y huesos, aire y agua,
    animado
    despierto

Uno más, flexible, estirado, su alcance extendiendo
    elevado a las alturas en expectativa
    arqueándose hacia adelante

En el último momento
sin aliento, en equilibrio sobre el vacío voluptuoso
    tiemblan, se tocan,
    alientos haciéndose uno
se convierten en un solo instrumento

hacen música.

2006

Not one eighth of a millimeter
    space enough
        unbounded
          extravagant
          uncontested
          unconditional

    for prairies of quarks and muons
    to find themselves locked in atomic attachment

Not one eighth of a millimeter
    from you, I am
        profligate
          spendthrift
          improvident

    imprudent enough to fill galactic silences
    shriek strings
    across the frozen black topography

    to grace the electrons of our nucleus

Not a molecule struck by lightning
      not one breath inhaled
      then released into planetary atmosphere
      not the thickness of thread is

between us

Only the length of that thread
      twisting
        stretching
          lengthening

to the necessary

infinity

Nothing between us
but this hour

2012

OLD GIFTS

I saved your gifts

    poetry

    flowers now dry

    tickles

    music

They are in the garden

I see them every day
when I go out to live my life.

VIEJOS REGALOS

Guardé tus regalos

    poesía

    flores ahora secas

    cosquillas

    música

Están en el jardín

Los veo todos los días
cuando salgo a vivir mi vida.

2006

ONE PATH HOME

Alone the old crane stands
In the morning stillness
Long feathers rustling amidst brittle stems
Eyes sweeping the sky
Considering the path home

2000

ONE PATH HOME
Sumi, Old Crane 40 x 58 inches, Detail (1.5 x 4 inches)
1977

HOME BOUND

straw of summer flowers
held immobile, upright in snow

dirt tracks a frozen river of mud
refreeze in ruts half a foot deep

blue berries weight juniper trees
lean fence posts pull wire
shadows across iced fields

white-whiskered crane alone
in morning stillness
long feathers amidst brittle stems
eyes sweep cloud-struck sky
one path home

2012

Real estate is easier than love.

We walk through the rooms
       full of someone else's life
       empty of us

We think of our couch here
       our books over there
       room for all the stuff
       our life has accumulated

We imagine
       loving each other
       in front of the window

We remember
       that we will fight in the kitchen
       and make up on the porch

And decide that we can live here.

2008

El inmobiliario es mas fácil que el amor.

Caminamos a través de las habitaciones
    completas de la vida de alguien más
    vacías de nosotros

Pensamos en nuestro sofá aquí
    nuestros libros allá
    espacio para todas las cosas
    que nuestra vida ha acumulado

Imaginamos
    que nos amamos
    delante de la ventana

Recordamos
    que vamos a luchar en la cocina
    y reconciliarnos en el porche

Y decidimos que podemos vivir aquí.

2008

APRON STORY

In the paint department the clerk wears an apron.
As she works each can open
her hip is marked with the rhythm of her hand
and with the rhythm of her customers

Every color, hope, plan
is on her apron
her pocket is covered with the colors of their dreams

What will be covered, blotted from sight, from memory?
What leftovers from another time
finally are obliterated?

What will the new key open?
Changing the locks as they change their life
      a new house
      new love
      old fear
      old sorrow?

What hope is in the bag
as they check out?

2007

En el departamento de pintura la empleada lleva un delantal.
Al abrir cada lata
su cadera es llevada por el ritmo de su mano
y por el ritmo de sus clientes

Cada color, cada plan, cada esperanza,
está en su delantal
su bolsillo está cubierto con los colores de sus sueños

¿Qué será cubierto, borrado de la vista, de la memoria?
¿Qué retazos de un otro tiempo
se eliminarán al final?

¿Qué va a abrir la llave nueva?
Cambiando las cerraduras como cambian sus vidas
    ¿ una casa nueva
    un amor nuevo
    un miedo antiguo
    un antiguo dolor?

¿Qué esperanza quedará en la bolsa
mientras ellos se dirigen a la salida?

2007

SECURITY

the pendent lodestar
     beckoning siren
perjured the moon
in its wobbly orbit

     celestial aldermen
stars traipse through
compassed trajectory
under the milky way's arms

*Note: This poem is part of a series, work composed only from the
"security words" of internet filters.*

2010

BEDTIME STORY

I was dreaming of aspens

    Of making a bed.

    He said it will look pretty

But it will never hold up like that.

I made a picture of a bed, he made a picture of a bed.

    Four almost straight posts at the corners

    Three long trees on the sides.

Head to rest heads against, foot to hold it together.

Tree trunks sanded, polished, waxed

    Knots smoothed away

    Until they were just shadows

Memories of the branches.

The aspen sawdust smelled

    Of forest sap

    And sprayed out from the saw

Catching in our hair and eyelashes and sweaty skin.

Some assembly required.

    The pieces are fitted together

    Not quite perfectly

The long rails turn of their own accord sometimes.

The first night the frame of head and foot and rails

    Sat on the floor around the mattress

    A crib for a new marriage

Next day the platform raised the quilted box

And dropped it again.

More support was drawn up,

    Modified, built.

    We asked ourselves,

"Would the center hold?"

Now this old bed glows with so many
                          polishings of wax

        Scratches gouged here and there

        Wood still soft

As if it has just been interrupted as it grew.

Glowing in the morning

        As early sun sends a knife of light into the room

Glowing at midnight

        As the moon changes from evening gold to
                          night white

Still holding together for now.

2002

All night we lie
          under our white comforter
          in the comfort of our white bed
     while the snow slides over the mountain

  and lies down over everything

In the morning the feeble sun
          glimmers down
          until the cloud-blanket
  begins to evaporate

  in great sheets of silence

2008

TRAFFICKING

At the light
clocks tick

Idling bodies shimmer through
glare, mob momentarily at rest

Flame-painted
remains rise in the heat

Antediluvian fossils
forgotten faces
undeciphered
volatile vapors
still

Now
the time
the indefinite sometime
has arrived

2013

NIGHT TABLE

Sky darkens.
Past the meridian
dusk eases its way.

Beside the bed
essentials crown the night table

clock lamp radio
novel
eyeglasses

small china pitcher with a sprig of lilac

panicles already drooping
like tired eyelids
a breath of the spring garden

tea in a china cup without a saucer

smelling of spices
faraway hills
journeys and dreams

pencil next to the leather notebook

scent of trees
whiff of the life they once had
waiting for a new life of words

a photograph

remembrance of a sweet day
the aspens afire
your smile alight

Sleep is temporary death

a few things
unremarked
awaken us to this life

2002

HOMECOMING

Night rain on the windows

Sage tea –
        steam drifting transparently –

slowly   slowly
releases its fragrance

Quiet together
at home

REUNIÓN

Lluvia nocturna en las ventanas

Té de salvia
        el vapor a la deriva –
        transparente –

lentamente
suelta su fragancia

Tranquilos juntos
en casa

1985

PARTITA

I   Coffee break

        they lean into the space between them
        faces illuminated with interest
        or pheromones
        they leave their coffee to grow cold

        he explains
                the phenomenological world
                materialist dialectics
                kama sutra

        blind to the world
                they take one breath,
                exhale,
                then one more

        deaf to all but one voice,
                bellies, breasts, crotch, hair,
                focused,
                limerance absolute

immeasurable, preposterous, unquenchable appetite
    ravenous for bone and skin
    avid for muscle, fat, blood
    finger pads on webbing of toes
    hair against breast, tongue edging earlobe

    voice in the valley
    notched between the ends of clavicles

the roar of alive

II   Lust

    He just wants

    dominion over money, mind, body, over piles of flesh
        ownership of toes, taste buds, hips
        ownership of thought, intention, ambition
        piles of stuff no one wants

    She holds hurt in her bones,
        in mind
        in dreams
        at the edge
        of fingernails
        scraping the soul

two, cancered with regret

shrunk into a teaspoon of sown salt.

III   Weight

    hard tumor of hurt

    No need for absolution

        unrequited
        untouched
        no amends

    left with fingers

    bent backward off open palms,
    calloused with unanswered forgiveness

2013

POSTAL SERVICE

Your unwritten letter

     Unstamped
     Unsealed
     Unfolded in my heart

Says nothing at all.

1987

TRAVELING

find yourself in front of snowy smoking mountains
brush out of your hair the dust of miracles
close your eyes in the face of the six-o'clock sun.

2006-15

sky snow

scumbled over the landscape
undulates under blue clouds

late sun
rose-red, lavender-lake

half the spectrum broken
over the roiled surface

defined by ivory-black ribbons
of frozen rivers

no bird dares the winter sky

this titanium cylinder
radiant in the stratosphere

flies high in the face of sense.

1991

CLIMBING MONTSERRAT

Climbing as the fog breaks up
getting wet
smelling of the clouds

SUBIR A MONTSERRAT

Subir cuando la niebla se aclara
mojarse
oler a las nubes

2003

FRENCH CHOCOLATE

Dark, light, milk, white
70–80–94%
      bars
      squares
      cubes
      sticks
Ten kinds of chocolate ice cream
Chocolate with
      almonds, filberts, raisins, prunes,
      raspberries, oranges, tangerines,
      wine, coffee, tea, chile

Chocolate makers
chocolate bakers
silver pots for chocolate
pretty pitchers for chocolate

Chocolate lace on chocolate cake
chocolate in huge cups with cream
chocolate over anything at all
chocolate everywhere

Doesn't anyone like vanilla?

2006

CHOCOLATE FRANCÉS

Oscuro, claro, con leche, blanco
70–80–94%
    barras
    cuadrados
    cubos
    palitos
Diez tipos de helado de chocolate
Chocolate con
    almendras, avellanas, pasas, ciruelas,
    frambuesas, naranjas, mandarinas,
    vino, café, té, chile

Chocolateros
pasteleros de chocolate
ollas de plata para chocolate
jarras bonitas para chocolate

Encaje de chocolate en pastel de chocolate
chocolate en tazas enormes con crema
chocolate sobre cualquier cosa
chocolate en todas partes

¿ Qué no le gusta a nadie la vainilla?

2006

In Altona, Manitoba

The sign by the roadside says

"The day of judgment is near!"

Right now
we are squinting in the sun,
opening our eyes
to see this day –

and judge it fine.

En Altona, Manitoba

La cartelera al lado del camino dice que

"¡El día de juicio se acerca!"

En este momento
entrecerramos los ojos en el sol
abriendo nuestros ojos
para ver este día –

y lo declaramos muy lindo.

2008

AT SANTA MARIA DEL MAR, BARCELONA

Body of light

    bends sharp on the shallow steps

    lies prone on the cold beautiful stone

    curls up the wall

      climbs the arch of heaven

2006-2013

School Days

First of September

Girls' hair blowing across their eyes
Boys proudly wearing t-shirts a little too small
Men with glasses and important briefcases
Women with babies and books
And seriousness on their laps

Promising lawyers, cool enterprisers
Passionate zoologists, precise French speakers
All dreaming

Couples and trios and quartets sit on the grass
Leaning toward and then away from each other
In a friendship-making dance

They talk about death and art and freedom and sex
And what kind of pizza to get

1987

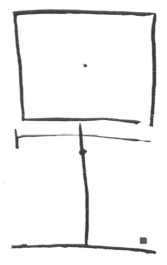

STAR
Sumi on handmade paper, 24 x 14 inches
1975

SIDEREAL

night draws each body
over moonless horizon

Jupiter rises

stars overwhelmed
orbit toward dawn

2003

BOX OF LIGHT

At six in the afternoon
The air is heavy with sun
Full with intimations of the coming evening
Still holding a lovely light

A motionless moment

I put my memories of the future
In this box of light.

CAJA DE LUZ

A las seis de la tarde-
El aire está pesado de sol
Lleno con intimaciones de la noche venidera
Aún teniendo una luz feliz

Un momento inmóvil

Pongo mis recuerdos del porvenir
En esta caja de de luz.

2006

DEAR FRIEND

Your voice reminds me
after so long a time
how sweet were our days together.
I love the memory of loving you.

I love you still.

QUERIDO AMIGO

Tu voz me recuerdas
después tanto tiempo
que dulce fueron nuestros días juntos.
Quiero la memoria de querrerte.

Aún te quiero.

2007

A NOTE FROM THE AUTHOR

The poems in this book were written over a period of more than four decades. I have often gone back and reconsidered the language or the ideas that have had a continuing allure for me. Where poems are in more than one language, I sought to capture the meaning, nuance and sound of the original rather than have a literal translation.

This book and much of my work for decades owes existence to the generosity and support from many sources. My profound gratitude to the New York Public Library, which granted me a year in the Allen Room at a critical time and helped to make the succeeding work possible. St. John's College, Santa Fe, unexpectedly suggested and produced a chapbook in 1998 to accompany an exhibition in their beautiful gallery. For precious time and encouragement my enduring thanks to Anderson Center at Tower View, Red Wing, MN; Artscape, Toronto, Canada; Maryland Institute College of Art Klots Residency, Rochefort-en-Terre, France; Wellspring House, Ashfield MA; Can Serrat, Barcelona, Spain; Air Vallauris, France; and Opus House, Truchas, NM.

I thank the poets who have entrusted their work to me. I have learned from all of them. For the friendship that came through poetry, thank you to Ann Filemyr, Kate Gale, Donald Levering, Denise Low, and Gary Worth Moody.

One more time, RD has insisted, mercilessly, that poetry is part of our life. This and all the books could not have been out in the world without him.

Susan Gardner
Santa Fe, 2015

Lifted to the Wind is set in Palatino,
a 20th century font designed by Hermann Zapf
based on the humanist typefaces of the Italian Renaissance and
named for the 16th century
Italian master of calligraphy Giambattista Palatino.